My Red Hat

Jill Larson Sundberg

CONARI PRESS

First published in 2004 by Conari Press,
an imprint of Red Wheel/Weiser, LLC
York Beach, ME
With offices at:
368 Congress Street
Boston, MA 02210
www.redwheelweiser.com

Typeset in ITC Officina Sans, Freestyle Script, and Bermuda LP Squiggle
by David A. Freedman.

ISBN: 1-57324-963-7

Printed in the United States of America
PC

11 10 09 08 07 06 05 04
8 7 6 5 4 3 2 1

The paper used in this publication meets the minimum requirements of
the American National Standard for Information Sciences-Permanence
of Paper for Printed Library Materials Z39.48-1992 (R1997).

$\mathcal{A}$cknowledgments

(Or . . . A Tip of "My Red Hat" to . . .)

I owe so much to so many wonderful people who have helped me achieve success with this first edition of *My Red Hat*.

JoAnn Hansen, my friend and colleague of Lakewood, Colorado, for years has been encouraging me to write something—anything—preferably a book. This one's for you, JoAnn. She also came up with the phrase, "My Red Hat puts a bounce in my step," which appears in this book.

Riley, Reeve, Braedy, Johannes, Linnea, Johnna, Annalise, and Erik—you have helped keep me young at heart, and you have shown me how much fun it is to be full of the dickens. You are all my little darlings.

Jodi and Paul Harvatin, Jeffrey Payant, Cindy Wall, Rick and Lisa Sundberg, and Karen Meyer, my dear children, for sharing my dreams and being supportive along the way. I love you all.

My mom and dad, Lois and Leonard Larson, who showed me what love is all about and how to have fun. Above all, thank you both for always being there for me.

My husband, Dick, for always encouraging me to be whatever I want and for giving me legal advice as needed (without billing me).

My cousin, lifetime friend, sister-at-heart, Bonnie Larson Kuslich, who is my confidant, my biggest fan, and my loudest cheerleader.

My brother, Michael, for encouraging me all along the way to get this book printed, for keeping me going when my type-A personality became bored or discouraged, for editing the book, and for organizing the pages.

My sister-in-law, Kay Larson, for keeping it all "under her red hat" until it came time to publish and for believing in me.

Group Grope classmates (Tom, Lowell, Bruce, Jane, Judy, and Bonnie) for caring about my day-to-day life and for sharing yours.

My dear friend, Barb Hendricks, who spent many days (and evenings) keeping everything organized and clean so that I could spend my time on the book.

Ellen Manakas, for being my friend through thick and thin and for appreciating me in spite of all my goofy antics, for giggling with me, sharing with me, and always, always believing in me.

Shelley Hohenecker of redhead DESIGN (who, by the way, is a lovely redhead), a fantastic illustrator, for coming up with the wonderful whimsical illustrations that she designed to look exactly like what I had in my mind. Aberdeen, South Dakota, can be proud of you, Shelley!

Jan Johnson of Red Wheel/Weiser/Conari, who brought this edition of *My Red Hat* into worldwide circulation. Jan is the first fairy godmother I have ever had in my life.

Bob Johnson of LithoTech in Bloomington, who guided me step-by-step through the first edition of my first book and who was kind enough to take each of my continuous phone calls and answer my never-ending questions.

Tim Anderson, who also helped answer all of my publishing questions.

Susan Egan, Kim Anderson, Jeanette LeDoux, Barb Hendricks, Bevy Hendricks, Peg Gallagher, Lisa McAlpin, and Ruby Hardina for your friendship and all of your hard work. You're the BEST!

Introduction

"Red Hat" clubs have sprung up all over the country, stirred by the Jenny Joseph poem, "Warning," which begins with the words, "When I am an old woman, I shall wear purple/With a red hat which doesn't go, and doesn't suit me."

I was introduced to Jenny Joseph's poem by Harpies' Bazaar, a wonderful gift shop in Mankato, Minnesota. The managers there suggested that I contact Sandra Martz, the owner of Papier Mache Press, to see if I might represent the book titled, *When I Am An Old Woman I Shall Wear Purple* to the gift market. I began selling that book to the gift industry in 1989 and the rest is history.

I had the pleasure of meeting Jenny Joseph a few years ago when she came to Minnesota for a visit filled with book signings and interviews. She was interviewed by Charlie Boone and Roger Erickson on WCCO Radio. She stayed at my home in Bloomington for a few days, and she was a delightful and extremely interesting guest.

It has been my pleasure to put together this edition of *My Red Hat*. I hope you will have as much fun reading it as I had compiling it.   —Jill Larson Sundberg

My Red Hat

gives me Joy!

My Red Hat

puts a

Bounce in my step.

My
Red Hat
gives me
confidence.

My Red Hat and I

have fun together.

My Red Hat

sets me

apart from the crowd.

My Red Hat
doesn't tell
any of my secrets.

My Red Hat
makes me
want to celebrate.

My Red Hat

never judges me.

My Red Hat

has helped me

meet many new friends.

(Some of them now

have Red Hats, too.)

My Red Hat
helps improve
a bad hair day.

My Red Hat

attracts much attention.

My Red Hat

makes

people

wonder what I have been up to.

My Red Hat

shares
my hurts.

My Red Hat

Hug

comforts me.

My Red Hat

protects me

from too much sun.

My
Red Hat
gives
me
class.

My Red Hat

will go anywhere
and everywhere with me,
regardless of
the time of day or night,
and won't ever go
without me.

My Red Hat

doesn't care

if I'm

30 – 40 – 50 – 60 – 70 – 80 –

90 – or 100.

Age makes no difference.

My Red Hat
doesn't care what I weigh.

My Red Hat
warms my soul.

My Red Hat

never says

a harsh word to me.

My
Red Hat
makes me
feel
special.

My Red Hat
brightens
a rainy day.

young at heart

My Red Hat
gets better with age.

My Red Hat
enriches my life.

My Red Hat

doesn't expect me to cook.

My Red Hat
stays beside me
when I'm sick.

My Red Hat
shares my lofty dreams.

My Red Hat

cheers me —— and cheers

others.

My Red Hat
doesn't care
what I wear.

My Red Hat

doesn't care

what my hair looks like —

whether or not

I have the latest style.

My Red Hat

never criticizes me.

My
Red Hat

goes

to the movies

with me.

My Red Hat
will run errands
with me.

My Red Hat

never complains to me.

My Red Hat
won't gossip.

My Red Hat
doesn't care
whether it's hot
or whether it's cold.

My
Red Hat
will go
shopping
all day
with me.

My Red Hat is the frosting on my outfits.

My Red Hat and I

make a great team.

My Red Hat
spends quality time
with me.

My Red Hat

gives me courage.

My
Red Hat
helps me
take
the world
by storm.

My Red Hat
makes me
the life of the party.

My Red Hat

broadens my horizons.

My Red Hat
will be with me forever.
We will be friends
for life.

My Red Hat and I
will grow old together!

Jill Larson Sundberg is proud to be the wearer of a Red Hat, a woman of a certain age, and a small-business woman, who runs Access Marketing Systems and sells gift items and books to retailers all over the Upper Midwest. She first encountered the idea of a Red Hat when she helped make the classic *When I Am an Old Woman I Shall Wear Purple* a bestseller. She lives outside Minneapolis.